Ery Nzaramba

Ery Nzaramba left Rwanda to settle in Belgium in 1994. Ten years later he moved to the UK for an acting career.

In 2014 Ery started working with director Peter Brook and long-time collaborator Marie-Hélène Estienne, featuring in world tours of *Battlefield* and *The Suit*.

Ery has been awarded two Grants for the Arts by Arts Council England and an Arvon Grant for his writing. He has written and directed short films; *Split/Mixed* is his first piece written for theatre. He wrote the first draft in 2013 and was invited to perform it in New York, Berlin and Belfast. The play continued to be developed and its current version premiered to critical acclaim at the Edinburgh Fringe Festival in 2016.

'Every time someone asks where I'm from, it's a reminder of how lucky and privileged I've been. In 1994 Rwanda was in the news for all the wrong reasons. It was being torn apart by a civil war and a genocide. Unlike millions of others who couldn't, my family escaped. Because we could. And we got all the support in the world because we were 'refugees'. But were we, really? Would I be able to look in the eye of one of the other millions of Rwandans who couldn't leave, and say "I'm a refugee"? I've lived in Europe for nearly a quarter of a century now, and though I'm no longer a refugee, that question has continued to haunt me. So, I decided to write Split/Mixed.*' – Ery Nzaramba*

First published in the UK in 2017 by Aurora Metro Publications Ltd.
67 Grove Avenue, Twickenham, TW1 4HX
www.aurorametro.com   info@aurorametro.com

Split/Mixed copyright © 2017 Ery Nzaramba
Cover photo and design copyright © Greg McKinney

Production: Simon Smith

With many thanks to: Marina Tuffier, Peter Fullagar, Abi Silverthorne and Anthony Crick.

Printed in the UK by 4edge Limited.
ISBNs:
978-1-911501-97-8 (print)
978-1-911501-98-5 (ebook)

SPLIT/MIXED

*A thought-provoking quest to find
a singular voice*

ERY NZARAMBA

AURORA METRO BOOKS

Maliza Productions

Maliza Productions was founded by Ery Nzaramba. 'Kuliza' means 'to make cry' in Kinyarwanda... so beautiful it makes you cry. Beauty, emotions, the clash of times and cultures... these are some of the qualities that Maliza productions for stage and screen aspire to explore.

Maliza Productions a été fondée par Ery Nzaramba. 'Kuliza' veut dire 'faire pleurer' en Kinyarwanda... tellement beaux qu'on en pleure. Beauté, émotions, choc des temps et cultures... voici quelques-unes des qualités que les productions de Maliza aspirent à explorer.

CONTENTS

SPLIT/MIXED   7

SPLIT/MIXED en francais   51

*For my little sister Jenny-Loïs,
my mum Marie-Thérèse, my dad Phocas*

For my little sister Maya

For Janika, Akira, Themba

For the Kinet family

SPLIT/MIXED

Split/Mixed has its Asian premiere at the Hong Kong World Cultures Festival in November 2017.

Directed by Jude Christian.
Sound design by Helen Skiera.
Lighting design by Katie Pitt.

PROLOGUE

Today, in a theatre.

Eddy walks on stage with a twin-deck cassette player from the 80s. He chooses a spot on stage and puts the player down, then greets the audience.

EDDY Hello. My name is Eddy Hamuleti. Thank you all for coming to my show. The play you're about to see is the story of a man from Rwanda living in the Diaspora. One day, he goes to a club in East London and meets a girl. They chat... they dance...

He presses PLAY on the ghetto blaster and a club song starts playing...

HERE AND NOW

A night club. Eddy impresses Chloe with his moves.

CHLOE *(laughs)* Wow! That's amazing! You're such a good dancer...!

EDDY   Thanks!

CHLOE   So where are you from?

EDDY   Wapping. How about you?

CHLOE   Dalston.

EDDY   O, we're practically neighbours...! Taking the bus tonight?

CHLOE *(smiles)* Maybe... *(A silent, awkward, shy, dance for a bit. Then–)* So, where are you from originally?

EDDY *(gets it)*   Oh, Rwanda.

CHLOE   Uganda?

EDDY   Ru-an-da.

CHLOE   Oh, Rwanda. Where's Rwanda?

EDDY   In Africa.

CHLOE *(rolls her eyes)* I know it's in Africa. I meant, where in Africa?

EDDY   Oh... At the heart of Africa, right below the equator.

CHLOE   Your English is pretty good.

EDDY   Thank you.

SURVIVOR'S DILEMMA

CONSCIENCE   Perfect time to move on to another subject, Eddy...

VANITY   No, tell her more...

CHLOE   So when did you leave Rwanda then?

CONSCIENCE   Lie!

VANITY   Tell her!

EDDY   In 1994.

Chloe thinks for a moment, then:

CHLOE   Hang on, wasn't there...?

EDDY   Yes.

CHLOE   Were you there?

CONSCIENCE   LIE!!

VANITY   TELL HER!!

EDDY *(to Chloe)*   Yes. I was there.

My reflection

A complexion

Plagiarised

In her eyes.

Hero

Zero

Freak

Bleak

Victim

Invictum.

The old image muddies

New colour new flavour

It is no longer Eddy's

It's of a genocide survivor.

HERO OR ZERO

VANITY   Cool. You're special. Unique. The survivor. You've seen shit. You are Othello to her Desdemona. A hero in a war film.

CONSCIENCE   Eddy, don't listen to Vanity. You're not a hero! You're not a genocide survivor!

Vanity stops the tape.

VANITY   He is a genocide survivor! And he's allowed to pull girls with his story! Like Othello!

CONSCIENCE   He has no right to do so, he's a fake!

VANITY   He escaped!

CONSCIENCE   He's a counterfeit!

VANITY   He lost people through the genocide!

CONSCIENCE   He's a phoney!

VANITY   He was a war refugee!

CONSCIENCE   A bogus!

VANITY   He could have been killed!!

CONSCIENCE   How can you feel sorry for him?! Must I remind you of his upbringing? *(Brandishes a tape)* My memory is intact!

Conscience goes to the cassette player, removes Eddy's tape, inserts his own and plays:

CONSCIENCE *(on tape)* Once upon a time, in the 80s to be precise, in a country far far away...

Rwanda, to be precise, an aeroplane hailing from Belgium lands on the tarmac of Rwanda national airport... And out steps a young boy called Eddy, his younger sister called Gabby, and their mother called... er... Mum.

RWANDA, THE MOTHERLAND

MUM	Gabby, give me your hand... Eddy, you too...
YOUNG EDDY	Very loud.
	Very hot.
	Smells funny.
	A foreign country.
	My country?
DAD	Eddy!!
YOUNG EDDY	Dad!
	He crosses the runway without harm
	Picks Gabby and I in his arms.
	Kisses Mum on the lips.
	Kisses us on the cheeks.
GABBY	You sting!
YOUNG EDDY	Kisses Gabby once more.
GABBY	Aaah!
DAD	Gabby...! Do I sting that much?!
GABBY	A fly!!
DAD	Ah... Of course. You'll have to get used to them Gabby. This isn't Belgium.

YOUNG EDDY   Dad, why did you have to leave last week?

DAD   I had to come and prepare our new home Eddy. Do you two know where we are?

YOUNG EDDY   No.

DAD   This is Rwanda. Where Mummy and Daddy were born.

Home.

YOUNG EDDY   And this is where Lil' Jenny is born *(Holds a baby in his arms)* She's God's grace–

GABBY   Don't look so scared, she's just a baby!

YOUNG EDDY   The gap from Gabby is six years. Primary school!

Conscience interrupts and fast-forwards the tape.

CONSCIENCE   Boring...

VANITY   Hey! That's the bit where he gets the caning of his life, that's important!

CONSCIENCE   No it's not. Just his introduction to Rwanda, that's all. Everybody knows everybody gets caned at school in Africa, it's no big deal.

VANITY   He was traumatised by the experience...

CONSCIENCE   So? Childhood trauma blah blah... 'S got nothing to do with what we're discussing here...

VANITY   Well according to Freud–

Conscience plays the tape.

CONSCIENCE *(on tape)*   Secondary school!

CONSCIENCE   That's it! Now shut up and listen…

MIXING IN WITH THE ELITE

YOUNG EDDY   Same youth, different rules.
We do not run, we walk
We do not speak, we talk
This school more than anywhere else.
Red, Yellow, Black
And I don't mean Belgium's flag
Mix with White and play tag
No we don't, though we could but instead
It's Hip Hop, Basketball, who's in whose bed
It's the International School of Kigali.
The most prestigious school in the country.

EDDY'S OTHER FAMILY

CHRIS   Edmundooo!
YOUNG EDDY   Chris.
My other half, my best friend.
We first met at primary school
When he was the new fish in the pool
After arriving from Europe with the same glow

That I had seven years ago.

He and I are middle class

Mixing in with the brass

Thanks to the education of our dads.

CHRIS   Hey I got the lyrics to 'Jump' by Kris Kross, wanna see them?

YOUNG EDDY AND CHRIS *(sing along)* '–And Mac Daddy make it up! Jump! Jump! Kris Kross make it up! Jump! Jump!' *(They break out laughing.)*

CHRIS   So! Who's it gonna be? Katia, Mireille or Nathalie? You should go for Katia. The girl loves you, everybody knows. Nathalie and Mireille... You can try but it's risky. Go for the easy option, go for Katia. I'll even help you write the letter!

YOUNG EDDY   O Chris.

In class, we sit together.

Out of school, we're at my place or his.

Talking girls

Writing them letters

Transcribing songs

Writing them as letters

Discussing our next haircut

(To Chris) Shall we do a Fresh Prince of Bel-Air?

– Shaved sides and a flat top –

Or a Bobby Brown?

– With a line cutting through –

One day I stop being Chris's best friend.

He starts seeing other people.

So at school I hang out with David:

Super cool, super talented

And Cassius:

Chubby

But so lovable and so huggable

He's everyone's darling.

At home

I play football in a local club

And Gerard and Simba

Though they're poor

Become my mates.

Gerard is a strong defender

Tough to beat

But you wouldn't guess cos he's always laughing

Especially with a beer in his hand.

GERARD   Eddy we, buy me a beer man...

(Eddy passes him the money)

Ey... Thank you!

(Roars with triumphant laughter)

YOUNG EDDY   Simba!

Simba lives for his football

Yet he sold me his boots...

But the next day he had a new pair!

What a wheeler-dealer!

But none of them is Chris.

God! I want my Chris back!

Home. Dad is fiddling with a TV set.

DAD   Eddy, can you operate this?

Young Eddy immediately finds the station.

YOUNG EDDY   Rwanda has just launched its first TV broadcast

And Dad has just bought a TV to boast about.

The first program on the medium

Is the President's 1993 New Year address

Which will be followed by a broad schedule

Consisting of the News and a film from the West

To fill the two hour evening only broadcast

From seven to nine pm – or half past.

A music competition show currently under the hammer

Will officially inaugurate the launch in the summer.

God has listened to my prayers!

We shall compete!

Yep, we.

Cos I know Chris will never say no.

And I'll ask David and Cassius too.

Cause we've got to be Four.

Boyz II Men are Four.

Okay! We need:
A recording studio
A rehearsal space
Matching Kris Kross gear
And a proper portfolio
And preparation phase
To perform without fear...
Phew...
How are we gonna do that?!

A car comes at speed and screeches to a halt.

The Godfather!
Can get anything with no bother!
His car
And attire
Are the clues!
Comes out of the blue
Comes to the rescue!

Stage. Music show televised live.

YOUNG EDDY *(dances and sings)* 'Everybody get down, cos we're so funky! D-E-double C's gonna get real busy!'

PRESENTER Ladies and gentlemen, in celebrating the launch of R.B.C. – Rwandan Broadcasting Corporation – this Music competition show has brought us musicians we all know and love. We also discovered new gems... Unfortunately there can only be one winner tonight. So... without further ado... the winner is... D.E.C.C...! The Kris Kross of Kigali!

YOUNG EDDY We step up to the stage
To collect our winner's wage.
We're on TV!
We're a family.
And I've won my Chris back.

EVERYONE GOT WET

Vanity stops the tape.

VANITY Alright, alright, I got it, so he had a privileged upbringing–

CONSCIENCE Privileged?! He went to the elite school in the country! I mean he was in a boy band for Christ's sake... And now he's feeling sorry for himself...?

VANITY But privilege doesn't come into it, the genocide touched every Rwandan, no matter their social background!

(Brandishes a tape) You know, I've got a pretty good memory too!

He inserts his own tape and plays:

A distant boom.

VANITY *(on tape)* When the plane carrying the president of the republic of Rwanda was shot down, the earth shook, a powerful storm broke, heavy rains and hails fell upon the small landlocked country

and everyone, rich, poor, small, tall...
everyone got wet...

END OF YOUTH

Home.

MUM Eddy? Are you awake?

YOUNG EDDY I wake up. What's up?
The way Mum stands in my doorway
Her tone of voice different in some way
I know something's up.

MUM Turn on your radio.

He turns the radio on.

NEWSREADER *Ejo nijoro, indege yari itwaye Prezida wa Republika Juvénal Habyarimana yararashwe. Abari bayirimo bose barapfa. Dusabye abantu bose kuguma mu rugo, kugeza aho tugiriye andi makuru.*

['Last night, the plane carrying the president of the republic, Juvénal Habyarimana, was shot down. There were no survivors. We urge everyone to stay home till we get further news.']

He switches the radio off.

YOUNG EDDY Daytime, militias hunt and kill!
Nighttime, guerillas come down the hill!
The sky is littered with red stars
The air is shattered with red blasts.

> One morning, our wall
> Is scarred with many a hole.
> Must have been a grenade.
> We've no guns we've no blade
> So, apart from Dad, who's pale
> We spend the nights in the corridor.

Conscience stops the tape.

CONSCIENCE   In the corridor of a mansion... While people around them are being hunted down by machete-wielding militiamen and being hacked to death... You see, that's my problem right there. He may have 'witnessed' the genocide but he didn't 'survive' it. He wasn't even targeted.

VANITY   Let's just hear my story out and then we can discuss. And this time, you shut up and listen!

He plays his tape.

VANITY *(on tape)* While the family's under siege, afraid to leave the house, sleeping on the floor in the corridor, George, Eddy's neighbour, also fifteen, never lets a day pass without checking on Eddy and his family...

THE FRIENDS ARE NO LONGER

GEORGE   Eddy!

YOUNG EDDY   Hey George!

GEORGE	*Bite*? ['How are you?']
YOUNG EDDY	Alright.
GEORGE	Did you hear about Cassius?
YOUNG EDDY	No...
GEORGE	He was killed. He came eye to eye with guerillas outside his house. And Victor, Edward, Emile, Justin, Rose, Yvonne... Gisèle! All killed by militias.
YOUNG EDDY	And David?
GEORGE	They've already left the country.
YOUNG EDDY	And...

Beat.

GEORGE	Chris...? Militias went to the house and sprayed the whole family with bullets.
YOUNG EDDY	I didn't know they were Tutsi...
GEORGE	I don't think they were... I think it was political... It's crazy man, so many people are being killed... Sometimes it's just jealousy or a grudge... Neighbour says you're Tutsi and that's it.
YOUNG EDDY	Or you're beautiful, rich... tall...
GEORGE	That doesn't mean you're Tutsi though, my brother's tall and he's not a Tutsi.
YOUNG EDDY	...How is he?
GEORGE	Shit scared. He won't leave the house.

MUM'S SECRET

Home.

MUM   Eddy, where are your sisters?

YOUNG EDDY   Jenny, Gabby and I

Gather round Mum in the dining room.

Dad's asleep.

Been getting worse lately.

Lost his voice lost his weight

The effort to speak and stand is too great.

So it's a strange thing to hear the tales

Of Dad wooing Mum back in the days.

Cause that's why Mum's gathered us today:

To tell us the story of their bygone days.

MUM   ...And when your father received a scholarship to study in Belgium, he instantly became a celebrity in the village. And from then on every time he came to visit me, well, my sisters were very jealous... When we got married he was still studying in Belgium so we went back together, where you two were born... Once there, I had a lot of cleanup to do: your Dad had had quite a few girlfriends and had kept the photos, letters... everything.

YOUNG EDDY   Suddenly

Mum changes the subject.

Mum

Says

She was adopted.

By a friend of her dad's.

When her own dad died.

That friend

– Granddad! –

Took her away from her own mum.

Mum doesn't know what happened to her Mum.

She's never seen her since.

MUM My... your granddad was rich and powerful, a diplomat, with two wives. And about fifteen children altogether. He thus decided I'd be better off with him, me being a poor Tutsi child...

Pause.

YOUNG EDDY Gabby, did you know about Mum? You didn't seem surprised...

GABBY I didn't, but it made sense to me.

YOUNG EDDY How?

GABBY You never noticed she looks nothing like our aunts? And I've always felt different around them.

YOUNG EDDY Yes, me too, but I always thought that was because we came from Belgium.

LIL' JENNY What are you two talking about?

GABBY You wouldn't understand Jenny, you're too young.

LIFE UNDER SIEGE

YOUNG EDDY Staying indoors

Is not expected.
You can be suspected
Of anything
At anytime
And on a whim.

Dad...
Can't do anything.
Mum...
Must stay in!
So I
From Boy to Man
Man of the clan
Man with a plan
Take the risks
Walk the streets.

Street.

GERARD   Eddy we! *Bite?*

YOUNG EDDY   I bump into Gerard.
Fifteen
Just like me
Yet I'm terrified.
He's high.
With an AK-47 on his back.

GERARD   D'you hear about Simba? (*Eddy shakes his head, negative.*)

We went in and cut them all. Oh, Simba escaped so we chased him through the thick vegetation round their house...

I'm the one who caught him! *(Roars with laughter.)*

Buy me a beer, man...

YOUNG EDDY   I... I've got no money...

Gerard's laughter vanishes.

GERARD   Where you going anyway?

YOUNG EDDY   I'm... just walking the streets...

With an extra glint in his eyes

He looks at me, high...

Middle-class

Handsome

– I got it from my mum –

I tick all the boxes!

After a loong stare...

GERARD   I'm going to the bar.

(Pointing to his Kalashnikov) Probably won't have to pay anyway. *(Roars with laughter.)*

YOUNG EDDY   I don't tick all the boxes after all... It must have been my height... The lack of it.

HIDING AND LEAVING

GEORGE   Eddy! We're leaving tomorrow. And with you. I'm not allowing our pickup truck to start without your family in it. Tell your parents.

MUM   George, *bite*?

GEORGE	I'm well Mama-Eddy, thank you.
MUM	Where will you take us?
GEORGE	We're going to my grandparents. We can drop you anywhere along the way.
MUM	Eddy, Gabby, Jenny, gather everything precious you've got.

Eddy's bedroom. He goes through a photo album:

YOUNG EDDY Katia, Mireille, Nathalie...

(Sighs) Chris...

My school album.

(Puts the album aside. Goes to his stereo. He suddenly presses play and breaks into dancing and singing to a mix of his favourite songs)

'And Mac Daddy make it up! JUMP! Jump! Kris Kross make it up! Jump! Jump!'

'BEAT IT! Beat it! Beat it! Beat it! No one wants to be defeated! Aw!'

'Although we've come to the END OF THE ROAD!'

(Breaks out of it as suddenly as he'd started)

... And my cassettes and stereo, and that's it.

(Puts cassettes and stereo aside)

A hole in the ceiling

I climb in

Our precious belongings

I stack them in.

GABBY   Are we even gonna get past the first road block, Eddy? Mum should make herself ugly. That way we'd have a chance. What about the maid, the nightguard and their baby boy? They're like family now. Will there be space for them in the car?

YOUNG EDDY   I don't know, Gabby!

The pickup truck is a twin cab and five-seater.

Mother's convinced Father:

MUM   We'll go to the nearest town, no farther.

Either way we cannot stay.

DAD *(with great difficulty)* Help me to the car then, I say.

YOUNG EDDY   So it's Mum and I

Each by his side

He agonises

The others sympathise

He gets inside.

Back seat:
Dad, Mum, lil' Jenny, George's mum.
Mum's doing her best to vanish.

Passenger seat:
George's eldest brother.
Wishing his height could diminish.

Driver's seat:
George.

Not one of his older brothers.
George.

In the truck-bed:
The rest of his family and precious items on their list
Gabby and I sitting in their midst.
Our maid and night guard and their baby boy
Will... stay.
And look after the house until we're back.

Road.

Road block.
Dead bodies on the road side.
Were they tall?
Were they rich?
Were they beautiful?
Did their ID have 'Tutsi' ticked?
They were cut by the militias.
Who inspect the rear.
And inspect the front.

MILITIAMAN   MUGIYE HE? MURIMO MURAHUNGA IKI?! KUKI MUHUNGA KIGALI?

ID!

['Where are you going? What are you fleeing? Why are you fleeing Kigali?

ID!']

YOUNG EDDY   One ID is missing, can he count?

As the militiaman hands back the IDs, he notices Eddy's mum. He points at her.

MILITIAMAN   *Uriya. Hanze.* ['That one. Out.']

YOUNG EDDY   It's a good thing I can't see Mum from where I'm placed

Terror must be contorting her beautiful face.

George

The Kid

Intervenes.

GEORGE   Her husband is dying... Look for yourself!

Militiaman leans in.

MILITIAMAN   *Hanze.* ['Out.']

YOUNG EDDY   Mum dives into her handbag and fishes out every bank note and coin she has. George hands them expertly to militiaman, no one else has seen, militiaman wants it all for himself:

MILITIAMAN   *(to the other militias, laughing)* ABA BA HUTU BAHUNGA! BAKANGA NO GUKORA AKAZI NKATWE! ['These Hutus running away! Who don't even want to 'work' like us!']

(To the car) MUGENDE! ['Go!']

He waves them through.

Conscience stops the tape.

CONSCIENCE   How was Mum allowed to live...? To this day, I still don't understand... Why wasn't she taken out of the car and

	raped and killed like the others whose bodies were piled on the side?
VANITY	You almost sound like you wish she'd been killed that day... O, that would have made you feel like a proper genocide survivor then, right?
CONSCIENCE	Don't be so stupid... But you've got to wonder. You never wondered?
VANITY	The money. 'S got to be the money.
CONSCIENCE	No... The money should have bought her at most a bullet in the head in the place of a machete on the neck... Remember our neighbours, they had even more money than we had...
VANITY	Dad looked like a dying man... Maybe they took pity on us...
CONSCIENCE	Militiamen having pity? You've got to be joking...
	I guess it was luck. God. Imana. Allah, Jehovah... Or whatever you want to call it. And that's exactly my point. It's either the money, help from the neighbour or sheer luck. Eddy didn't actually see Death in the eye.
VANITY	...Right.
	Shall we... carry on with my memory? Do you mind...?

Vanity plays the tape.

VANITY (*on tape*) George drops us in the neighbouring town of Gitarama and they go.

Good byes are quick, we'll meet again, we know.

PARADISE LOST

Compound.

YOUNG EDDY   Our host for now and a foreseeable future
Is a family's friend, a public figure.
There are other friends and relatives
All running away from killers and thieves.

One of the boys is tall and handsome
Which will make my work bothersome
For the girls are Rwandan beauties!
Not allowed on the streets.

Naomi stands out...

Naomi, my dream!
Looking at her is my treat!
She's seven years older
Which makes my resolve stronger!

Naomi and I, and the other pairs
Flirt...
And play checkers...
Flirting...
And collect waters
Ladies as well as geezers.
It's romantic
It's fantastic
It's hedonistic

It's– *(Remote explosions)*

Fireworks!! There, at the top of the hill!

We're young and in love...

So we run up the hill!

Top of the hill.

NAOMI Eddy we? Where are you?

YOUNG EDDY *(was playing a trick on her)* Ha ha, here, Naomi, hold my hand. *(They push their way through the gathered crowd)* Excuse me, sir...

SPECTATOR #1 *EY! Aba bana ra! Murimo murasunikira iki?* ['Eh! What's wrong with these kids! Why are you pushing?']

YOUNG EDDY We just wanna get to the front, we're young, and short... Come, Naomi. *(Ploughs forward)* Excuse me, sir...

SPECTATOR #2 *Ey! Ubu se murakora iki hano?? Mutahe, mutahe... Abana b'ubu rwose...* ['Eh! What are you doing here?? Go home, go home... Kids today really...']

YOUNG EDDY But why? We just–

NAOMI Eddy, maybe we should just stand here...

YOUNG EDDY No! Can you see anything from here? Neither can I. Let's go to the front. See what this fuss is all ab...

(They've reached the front)

Church yard.

Full of.

Bodies.
Old men, Women, Kids, Babies.
Smoke still lingers in the air
From the grenades that were thrown
in the pack.
It's cut by the killers' glare
Who rove through the bodies on the
rack.
On the look out
For that whimper
That budge
That would give away a body as still
alive.

Naomi and I are watching, how? Why?

A woman with a baby has budged.
No!! Don't move don't groan resist the
pain!!

An old man raises his arm
Begging
(A killer takes the old man's hand.
Cuts it off. Brandishes it to the crowd.
Hacks the rest of the body.
The woman's baby starts to cry.
The killer stops the hacking and goes
to the woman and her baby.
His machete goes up–)
Naomi and I force our way back
through the crowd–

SPECTATOR #3 *Aba bana barwaye iki ra?!* ['What is wrong with these kids?!']

YOUNG EDDY Back down the hill where we came from.

LOSS AND SOLACE

YOUNG EDDY Life resumes in the village.

Cousin Luke takes me out for a beverage.

When an errand boy finds us in the bar
We leave our gourds, head back in the dark.

We near the house and Cousin Luke's practically running.

We approach the house and through the air comes singing.

Compound.

Mum is sitting amongst the singing women.

Dad...

His bed fills the room.
His body is lit by a single candle.
I ignore the gloom
Touch his cold face and stumble...
He's really gone. What were his last words
Did he speak at all?

I'm drunk – with the dirge
Ignore the hum!
Find Mum.
A moment with my mummy.

Instead I find Naomi.

The night I lost my father
The night I lost my flower.

LEAVING IT ALL BEHIND

Car.

YOUNG EDDY   We're leaving everything and Daddy behind.
I'm leaving everything and Naomi behind.

We reach the main boulevard
Cousin Luke stops the car.

COUSIN LUKE   Let's think...
Let's... pray and prepare...

YOUNG EDDY   ...My tall Cousin Luke...
And my beautiful mum...
Only a miracle could save us.

A car appears at speed and screeches to a halt.

The Godfather!
Can get anywhere with no bother!
His car
And attire

Are the clues!
Always comes out of the blue
Always comes to the rescue!

On the road.

Road block.
Militiamen dance and swagger.

The Godfather
Powers his horn
Lowers his window
And bellows...

GODFATHER   ZAMURA IYO BARIYERI CYANGWA MBINJIREMO MWESE! ['Remove the roadblock or I drive through you all!']

YOUNG EDDY   He is louder than his horn!
It's not shouting
It's barking!

GODFATHER   WOOF! WOOF! WOOF! WOOF! WOOF!! ABA BASWERA NYINA NTIBUMVA RA? HAWUSIKILIYE?? ZAMURA IYO BARIYERI!! ['Don't these motherfuckers understand? Don't you understand?? Remove that roadblock!!']

YOUNG EDDY   Not slowing down.
Cousin Luke
Follows suit.

There's gonna be a carnage.
On top of the other carnage.

Then... just like that... they clear the way!

Wow.

Was this how we were supposed to do it all along?

Compound.

THE EXODUS

YOUNG EDDY　We join the extended family at the grandparents
In Gisenyi.
And together
Dots in the crowd
We slither
Across the border
And into Goma
Seek shelter
Stay together.
The new militia
Dysentery and Cholera
Raid our settlement
Kill and keep us in bondage
Hold me and my aunt hostage.
She's on a drip
I'm on a shit
I shit blood
Sweat out my flesh

Sit and lay on my bones.
They spare lil' Jenny
Usually illness-prone.
And ignore Mum and Gabby.
I survive.

Vanity stops the tape.

CONSCIENCE   Okay… Okay. I admit. It wasn't a stroll in the park.

VANITY   And privilege and money and all that shit… Don't come into it.

CONSCIENCE   Indeed indeed… They don't.

VANITY   Aha!

CONSCIENCE   It still doesn't give him the right to victimise himself though…

VANITY   God you're so stubborn!

CONSCIENCE   Oh am I…? Okay once in Goma, who did we meet…? I wonder whether you remember that too…

He plays the tape.

Street.

CHRIS *(on tape)*   Edmundoooo!!

YOUNG EDDY   It can't be. I look left, I look right, in front and behind but see nothing.

CHRIS   Edmundoooo!!

YOUNG EDDY   Could it be? On top of that truck, fully loaded, waving at me?

CHRIS   I'll jump off round the corner!!

YOUNG EDDY   I run after the truck to keep it in my view. The truck turns, I lose it. Faster!! Turn… No truck.

CHRIS   Edmundo!!

YOUNG EDDY   It IS him.

Chris.

My brother.

He crosses the road

Running

Smiling

We hug.

CHRIS   You've made it too man...!

YOUNG EDDY *(to himself)* How?! How!! How.

CHRIS   Listen man, I'm in touch with friends in Germany... I'm going there soon. How about you, how's it looking?

YOUNG EDDY   Mum is in touch with my uncle in Belgium who's trying to get us there.

We're lost for words.

Eventually

For he must have read the curiosity in my eyes

He tells me.

CHRIS   We were all in the living room when they came. I mean, I wasn't, I was in the toilet. They must have been in a hurry because they didn't search the house after they'd... finished. I stayed in the house for nearly a week before leaving. On foot. Though sometimes I did get a lift. I arrived here in Goma two weeks ago and the first thing I did was look for a telephone...

Conscience stops the tape.

CONSCIENCE Granted, Chris also had a privileged upbringing, but he lost everyone and everything. Eddy still had his family after the genocide. Dad doesn't count, he wasn't killed, he died of an illness. He would have died anyway.

VANITY You're working too hard to make Eddy feel guilty for surviving the genocide.

CONSCIENCE You're working too hard to make Eddy feel proud for witnessing the genocide.

VANITY I'm his vanity, that's my job.

CONSCIENCE And I'm his conscience.

VANITY Exactly! And you're supposed to guide him! Not to pop up every time he's performing his love story of a black man and a white woman meeting in an East London club! He's never once got to the end of the play. Ever! He's got to move on...

CONSCIENCE Look, I understand your frustration. But I honestly believe that Eddy must first learn to appreciate what he's been given. He now lives in Europe, where he's had a great education, where he can be anything he wants – the guy is an actor for crying out loud! So as much as I hate saying this, Eddy is, really, a genocide... beneficiary – if anything. As for the rest... He'll move on. If he, if we, let Time do its work.

(*To Eddy*) Did you hear that, Eddy...? Eddy! Did you hear what I said...? ED–

Eddy shakes Conscience and Vanity away.

We find Eddy back in the midst of his 'one-man play about a black man and a white woman meeting in an East London club', dancing with Chloe (beginning of the play).

Though he's got rid of his inner voices, he's still lost in thoughts, or, rather, in his past... This time, it is his own memory...

THE UNBURIED MEMORY

YOUNG EDDY Belgium.
A week since we arrived!
A week where nights turned bright!
A week free of blues!
A week full of fresh bread and juice!
Yeah, I've put on ten k's.
That's more than one k per day!

The Asylum Seekers' Centre:
Our new home, our shelter!
Fellow wannabe refugees:
Our new family!

The family room.

YOUNG EDDY Gabby, I, Mummy
– Where's Lil' Jenny? –
Sit on the bed
Mum strokes our heads.

MUM   Jenny and I have AIDS. I've had strong
                       suspicions all along and now tests have
                       confirmed we are seropositive.

YOUNG EDDY Mum and Jenny are dying?
                Why?
                How?

                Dad!

                But Jenny's eight years old
                How could she live this long
                And Goma
                The cholera
                How did she – how did they survive?

                Why us?
                Why JENNY?

                Dad!!

                Mum's crying.
                Gabby's crying.
                I...

                But where are my tears?

                How long till...?

                It's a Countdown.

LIVING AGAINST THE CLOCK

YOUNG EDDY Summer break and I work on a farm far from the centre.

Mum is proud to see me get my first job ever.

Asylum Seekers' Centre.

I bought Lil' Jenny
The grey roller-skates
She's been wanting.
I see her through the bars of the gate
She's busy counting.
She sees me
Stops her game
Calls out my name
Comes running
All smiling
Leaps into my arms
And I hold her
Tight.

She's lighter.
Thinner.

THE EXCURSION

MUM'S FRIEND *Ça vous dirait une petite excursion à Bruxelles?* ['What do you say to a little trip to Brussels?']

YOUNG EDDY	A friend of Mum's, met at the hospital Wants to take us on a trip to Brussels. Wants to make Mum's last days on earth as happy as possible. I hate it. Reminds me Mum's living her last days on earth. I can't do it. So Lil' Jenny, Gabby, and Mummy Visit our old schools, old homes and landmarks Come back with photos and joy in their hearts.

THE FIRST STRIKE OF THE CLOCK

Class.

REGISTRAR	*Bonjour tout le monde...* ['Good morning everyone...']
YOUNG EDDY	I'm in the class and the Registrar has just walked in.
REGISTRAR	Mr André... Do you mind if I steal Eddy for a minute?
YOUNG EDDY	I'm leaning against the wall, waiting.
REGISTRAR	Er... Eddy... Er...
YOUNG EDDY	I wouldn't want to be in his place.
REGISTRAR	Eddy... Your mum just passed. Your uncle's coming to pick you up. You

need to get ready. I'll pick up your stuff in the class, okay? Ça va Eddy...?

Asylum Seekers' Centre.

YOUNG EDDY   I look at the photos.

Mummy, Gabby, Jenny.

Her last days.

And I'm not there.

Wasn't there for Dad's last days.

Wasn't there for Mum's last days.

But where are those tears?!

THE LAST STRIKE OF THE CLOCK

YOUNG EDDY   Countdown's still counting down.

Lil' Jenny can't use her roller skates now.

Hospital.

She can't leave her hospital bed now.

The disease is eating her away

Yet we talk and play

She speaks differently, like a grown-up

As if her brain had decided to speed up

To give her those years it knows she'll never have.

(To Jenny and Gabby) I need the toilet, I'll be right back.

LIL' JENNY   I would have let you use my toilet but hospital rules stipulate that guests and patients ought not to share the toilet.

YOUNG EDDY   I know, I know. I'll go to another one.

LIL' JENNY   There's one down the hall on your right.

Toilet.

YOUNG EDDY   I pull the plug and flush away my tears.

Those tears I couldn't find

That's why

Was saving them for now.

Back in Jenny's room.

Hey I'm back.

GABBY   Jenny said you always take ages in the toilet... Well, she was right!

YOUNG EDDY   They laugh.

Both of them.

A hundred and fifty days after Mum's departure, Lil' Jenny has had enough of the fight and joins Mum and Dad.

The countdown stops at six hundred and two days.

She was nine.

HERE AND NOW

Eddy's memory stops.

He got lost in his past and forgot about his one-man show...

He goes to the tape recorder, puts Conscience's and Vanity's memories (tapes) away.

He becomes aware of the audience and so decides to give his one-man show another go. He rewinds his own tape (that of his one-man show) to the beginning, and plays.

A club song starts playing...

A night club. Eddy impresses Chloe with his moves.

CHLOE *(laughs)* Wow! That's amazing! You're such a good dancer...! So where are you from?

EDDY Wapping. How about you?

CHLOE Dalston.

EDDY O, we're practically neighbours...! Taking the bus tonight?

CHLOE *(smiles)* Maybe... *(A silent, awkward, shy, dance for a bit. Then–)* So, where are you from originally?

EDDY *(gets it)* Oh, *Belgium.*

Black out.

The End.

Split/Mixed has received support from many friends along the way. I'd like to thank them for contributing, in one way or another, to *Split/Mixed's* journey from its inception to what it is today. A special thank you to Donald Molosi, Gabriele Dionisi, Nyasha Hatendi, Alina Serban, Flora Veit-Wild, Zoe Norridge, Fin Kennedy, Tamasha Theatre, Soho Theatre, Voichita Judele, Jef Mitchell, Kivu Ruhorahoza, Ada Cotton, Unicorn Theatre, Marie-Hélène Estienne, Emily Gray, Trestle Theatre, Agnès Courtay, Carole Karemera. And thank you to my creative team, Helen (there from day one and counting!), Jude and Katie. Thank you for believing in the project.

Split/Mixed a reçu le soutien de beaucoup d'amis tout le long de son parcours. J'aimerais les remercier pour avoir contribué, d'une façon ou d'une autre, à l'aventure *Split/Mixed*, depuis ses commencements à ce qu'il est devenu aujourd'hui. Merci particulièrement à Donald Molosi, Gabriele Dionisi, Nyasha Hatendi, Alina Serban, Flora Veit-Wild, Zoe Norridge, Fin Kennedy, Tamasha Theatre, Soho Theatre, Voichita Judele, Jef Mitchell, Kivu Ruhorahoza, Ada Cotton, Unicorn Theatre, Marie-Hélène Estienne, Emily Gray, Trestle Theatre, Agnès Courtay, Carole Karemera. Et merci à mon équipe, Helen (là depuis le premier jour et toujours là!), Jude et Katie. Merci de croire au projet.

*À ma petite sœur Jenny-Loïs,
ma maman Marie-Thérèse, mon papa Phocas*

À ma petite sœur Maya

À Janika, Akira, Themba

À la famille Kinet

SPLIT/MIXED

Split/Mixed a sa première en Asie au World Cultures Festival à Hong Kong, en Novembre 2017.

Mise-en-scène de Jude Christian.
Son de Helen Skiera.
Lumière de Katie Pitt.

PROLOGUE

Aujourd'hui. Dans un théâtre.

Eddy Hamuleti entre avec une radio-cassette des années 80. Il repère un endroit et place l'appareil. Puis il salue le public.

EDDY Bonsoir. Je m'appelle Eddy Hamuleti. Merci à vous tous d'être venu à mon spectacle. La pièce que vous allez voir, est l'histoire d'un jeune homme provenant du Rwanda et vivant dans la Diaspora. Un jour, il va dans une boîte à Paris et rencontre une fille. Ils causent... ils dansent...

Il lance la bande et le dernier tube s'échappe des enceintes...

ICI & MAINTENANT

Une boîte. Eddy impressionne Chloé avec ses pas de danse.

CHLOÉ *(rie)*   Ouah! Non, mais, t'es un vrai génie de la danse, toi!

EDDY   Merci!

CHLOÉ   Au fait... Tu viens d'où?

EDDY   De La Chapelle. Et toi?

CHLOÉ   De La Villette.

EDDY   Ah bon, mais on est pratiquement voisins...! Tu prends le métro tout-à-l'heure?

CHLOÉ *(sourit)*   Peut-être... *(Un petit moment de danse gênée et timide. Puis–)* Au fait, je voulais dire, tu viens d'où d'origine?

EDDY *(comprend)* Ah, du Rwanda.

CHLOÉ   Uganda?

EDDY   Ru-an-da.

CHLOÉ   Ah, Rwanda. Tiens, c'est où encore le Rwanda?

EDDY   En Afrique.

CHLOÉ *(roule des yeux)* Je sais bien que c'est en Afrique. Je voulais dire: où, en Afrique?

EDDY   Ah... Au cœur de l'Afrique, juste en dessous de l'équateur.

CHLOÉ   Tu parles très bien français.

EDDY   Merci.

DILEMME DU SURVIVANT

CONSCIENCE   C'est le moment idéal pour changer de sujet, Eddy...

VANITÉ   Non, dis-lui plus...

CHLOÉ   Du coup, quand est-ce que t'as quitté le Rwanda alors?

CONSCIENCE   Mens!

VANITÉ   Dis-lui!

EDDY   En '94.

Un moment de réflexion pour Chloé, puis:

CHLOÉ   Attends, y a pas eu...?

EDDY   Si.

CHLOÉ   Tu y étais?

CONSCIENCE   MENS!!

VANITÉ   DIS-LUI!!

EDDY *(à Chloé)*   Oui. J'y étais.

Dans son regard

Mon reflet

Un plagiat

Complet.

Héro

Zéro

Incroyable

Pitoyable

Victime, cible

Invincible.

Une nouvelle image se cristallise

Nouvelle couleur

Nouvelle saveur

Elle n'est plus celle d'Eddy

Mais celle d'un survivant du génocide.

HÉRO OU ZÉRO

VANITÉ   Cool. T'es spécial. Unique. Un survivant. Parce que tu viens de loin. Tu es son Othéllo et elle ta Desdémone. Un héro de film de guerre.

CONSCIENCE   Eddy, n'écoute pas Vanité. T'es pas un héro! T'es pas un survivant du génocide!

Vanité arrête la cassette.

VANITÉ   Il est survivant du génocide! Et il a le droit de draguer avec ses histoires! Comme Othéllo.

CONSCIENCE   Il n'en a pas le droit, il est faux!

VANITÉ   Il s'est échappé!

CONSCIENCE   Une contrefaçon!

VANITÉ   Il a perdu des gens à cause du génocide!

CONSCIENCE   Un imposteur!

VANITÉ   Il était réfugié de guerre!

CONSCIENCE   Un bidon!

VANITÉ   Il aurait pu être tué!

CONSCIENCE   Vraiment? Comment peux-tu avoir pitié de lui?! Dois-je te rappeler son enfance? *(Brandit une cassette)* Ma mémoire est intacte! *(Conscience va* *au lecteur, retire la cassette d'Eddy, insère la sienne et joue.)*

CONSCIENCE *(sur cassette)* Un jour, dans les années 80 pour être précis, dans un pays très, très, lointain... le Rwanda, pour être précis, un avion provenant de la Belgique atterrit sur le goudron surchauffé de l'aéroport international du Rwanda... Descendirent alors, du dit avion, un jeune garçon appelé Eddy, sa petite sœur appelée Gabby, et leur mère appelée... euh... Maman.

RWANDA, LA PATRIE

MAMAN   Gabby, donne-moi ta main... Toi aussi, Eddy...

JEUNE EDDY   Hyper bruyant.

Hyper-méga chaud.

Ça sent le pourri.

Étrange, ce pays.

Mon pays?

PAPA   Eddy!!

JEUNE EDDY   Papa!

Il traverse la piste sans problème

Nous prend dans ses bras, Gabby et moi-même.

Sur la bouche de Maman, un bisou

La même chose pour nous, mais sur la joue

GABBY	Tu piques!
JEUNE EDDY	Et un autre bisou pour Gabby.
GABBY	Aaah!
PAPA	Gabby...! Je pique tant que ça?!
GABBY	Une mouche!!
PAPA	Ah... Alors là, va falloir que tu t'habitues, Gabby. On n'est pas en Belgique ici.
JEUNE EDDY	Papa, pourquoi t'as dû partir la semaine passée?
PAPA	Fallait que je vienne préparer notre nouvelle maison, Eddy. Vous savez où on est, vous deux?
JEUNE EDDY	Non.
PAPA	Ici c'est le Rwanda. Là où sont nés Maman et Papa.

À la maison.

JEUNE EDDY	Et c'est ici que naît Petite Jenny. *(Tient un bébé dans les bras)* C'est un cadeau de Dieu.
GABBY	N'aie pas peur, ce n'est qu'un bébé!
JEUNE EDDY	L'écart entre elle et Gabby est de six ans.
	École primaire!

Conscience avance la bande.

CONSCIENCE	On s'en fout...
VANITÉ	Hé! C'est le moment où il reçoit la raclée de sa vie, c'est important!
CONSCIENCE	Non, ça ne l'est pas. C'était juste son introduction au Rwanda, rien de plus. Tout le monde sait que les élèves sont

punis à coups de bâtons en Afrique, c'est rien de spécial.

VANITÉ   L'expérience l'a complètement traumatisé.

CONSCIENCE   Et alors? Traumatisme d'enfance bla bla bla... Rien à voir avec notre discussion...

VANITÉ   Eh bien pourtant d'après Freud—

Conscience joue la bande.

CONSCIENCE *(sur cassette)* École secondaire!

CONSCIENCE   Voilà! Maintenant ta gueule et écoute...

FRÉQUENTER L'ÉLITE

JEUNE EDDY   Même jeunesse

Mais on progresse.

On ne court pas, on pose

On ne crie pas, on cause

Surtout dans ce foutoir.

Rouges, Jaunes et Noirs

Et je ne parle pas du drapeau belge

Fréquentent Blancs et font Beige

En jouant au Cache-cache – je rigole

C'est plutôt Hip-Hop, Basket, qui couche avec qui à l'école

C'est le Lycée Internationale de Kigali.

La plus prestigieuse institution du pays.

L'AUTRE FAMILLE D'EDDY

CHRIS   Edmundooo!

JEUNE EDDY   Chris.

Mon autre moitié, mon meilleur ami.

On s'est rencontré à l'école primaire

Quand il était encore tout débonnaire

Ayant débarqué de l'Occident

Tout sage et tout pensant

Comme je l'étais, il y a sept ans.

Lui et moi sont deux petits bourgeois

Fréquentant les Grands Bourgeois

Grâce à l'éducation de nos pères qui ont montré la voie.

CHRIS   Hé j'ai les paroles de ‹Jump› de Kris Kross, t' veux voir?

JEUNE EDDY ET CHRIS (*chantent*) ‹...And Mac Daddy make it up! Jump! Jump! Kris Kross make it up! Jump! Jump!›

Ils se marrent.

CHRIS   Alors? Ce sera qui? Katia, Mireille ou Nathalie? Vas pour Katia, mec, la meuf t'adore, tout le monde sait. Mais Nathalie ou Mireille... Tu peux toujours essayer mais c'est risqué. Te complique pas la vie, vas pour Katia. Je peux même t'aider à écrire la lettre si tu veux!

JEUNE EDDY   Ah Chris.

En classe, on est assis côte-à-côte.

Si pas en classe, lui ou moi est l'hôte

Et nous parlons de nos amours
Leur écrivons des lettres
Jouant les Prophètes...
Nous recopions des chansons d'amour
Les présentons comme étant nos lettres
Jouant les Poètes...
Nous décidons de notre prochaine coupe
(*À Chris*) Et si on se faisait un ‹Prince de Bel-Air›?
– Coupe carrée, les côtés rasés –
Ou peut-être un ‹Bobby Brown›?
– Avec une raie au milieu –

Un jour, comme ça, Chris et moi ne sommes plus meilleurs amis.
Il commence à voir d'autres gens.
Alors au Lycée moi je fréquente David:
Super cool, bourré de talents
Et Cassius:
Gros
Mais si adorable et si doux et moelleux
Il est le chouchou de tout le monde.
À la maison
Je joue au foot dans l'équipe du quartier
Et Gérard et Simba
Même s'ils sont pauvres
Deviennent mes potes.

                    Gérard est dur comme défenseur

                    Dur à battre

                    Pourtant tu le devinerais jamais en le
                    voyant

                    Il rit tout le temps

                    Surtout quand il a une bière dans les
                    mains.

GÉRARD   Eddy we, achète-moi une bière s'il te
                    plaît... *(Eddy lui passe de la monnaie)*
                    Ey... Merci...!

Et éclate d'un rire triomphant.

JEUNE EDDY   Simba!

                    Simba vit, dort et mange football.

                    Pourtant l'autre jour il m'a vendu ses
                    crampons...

                    Et le lendemain il avait une nouvelle
                    paire!

                    Quel magouilleur!

                    Mais aucun d'eux n'est Chris.

                    Mon dieu! Qu'est-ce que je voudrais
                    retrouver mon Chris!

À la maison. Papa est en train de tripoter la télé.

PAPA   Eddy, tu sais comment ça marche?

Eddy trouve immédiatement la chaîne.

JEUNE EDDY   Le Rwanda vient de lancer sa toute
                    première chaîne de télé

                    Et Papa vient d'acheter un poste sur
                    lequel se vanter.

La toute première émission prévue sur
les ondes

Est le discours de nouvel de 1993 par
le président

Qui sera suivi d'une programmation
ciblée à la ronde

Consistant du Journal et d'un film
provenant de l'Occident

Pour remplir les deux heures de
diffusion, rien que le soir

Entre sept et neuf heures du soir

– Ou neuf heures et demie.

Pour célébrer l'événement

Un concours de musique télévisé

En conception, actuellement,

Aura lieu cet été.

Dieu a répondu à mes prières!

Nous allons participer!

Oui, nous.

Parce que je sais que Chris ne dira
jamais non.

Et je demanderai aussi à David et
Cassius

Il faut qu'on soit Quatre.

Boyz II Men sont Quatre.

Alors... Nous aurons besoin:

D'un vrai studio

D'une salle de répétition

> De fringues à la Kris Kross
> D'un vrai portfolio
> Et d'une phase de préparation
> Afin de jouer à la Kris Kross...
> Ouah...
> Comment on va faire?!

Une voiture arrive à toute vitesse et freine avec crissement.

> Le Parrain!
> Qui peut tout avoir sans problèmes!
> Y a qu'à voir sa caisse – ses fringues même!
> Sort de nulle part
> L'homme de sauvetage!

Salle de concert. L'événement est télédiffusé en direct.

JEUNE EDDY (*danse et chante*) ‹Everybody get down, cos we're so funky! D-E-double C's gonna get real busy!›

PRESENTATEUR TV Mesdames, Mesdemoiselles et Messieurs! Tout en célébrant le lancement de TR1 – Télévision Rwandaise Numéro 1 – ce spectacle, ce concours de musique, nous a permis d'apprécier des musiciens que nous connaissons tous et que nous aimons tous. Mais aussi de découvrir des nouvelles perles... Malheureusement il ne peut y avoir qu'un seul gagnant ce soir. Et donc... sans trop tergiverser... les vainqueurs, ce soir sont... D.E.C.C...! Les Kris Kross de Kigali!

JEUNE EDDY Nous montons les marches de marbre

Pour recevoir le prix d'Art.
Nous sommes des stars.
Nous sommes inséparables.
Et j'ai retrouvé mon Chris.

TOUT LE MONDE FUT MOUILLÉ

Vanité arrête la bande.

VANITÉ Okay, okay, j'ai bien compris, il a eu donc une enfance privilégiée-

CONSCIENCE Privilégiée?! Il était à l'école d'élites! M'enfin, il a même fait partie d'un Boy Band... Et maintenant il se plaint...?

VANITÉ Mais c'est pas une question de privilège, le génocide a touché tout Rwandais quel que soit son milieu social! *(Brandit une cassette)* J'ai aussi une bonne mémoire tu sais!

Il introduit sa cassette et joue:

Sur cassette:

Un ‹boum› lointain.

VANITÉ *(sur cassette)* Quand l'avion transportant le président de la république du Rwanda fut abattu, la terre trembla, un orage puissant amena des pluies et grêles violentes sur ce petit pays enclavé, et tout le monde, riches, pauvres, petits, grands, minces, gros... tout le monde fut mouillé...

FIN DE L'ENFANCE

À la maison.

MAMAN   Eddy? T'es réveillé?

JEUNE EDDY   Je me réveille – qu'est-ce qu'il y a?

La façon dont Maman se tient dans l'embrasure de la porte

Et le ton de sa voix qui me trouble en quelque sorte

Me disent que quelque chose ne va pas.

MAMAN   Allume ta radio.

Il allume sa radio.

PRESENTATEUR RADIO *Ejo nijoro, indege yari itwaye Prezida wa Republika Juvenal Habyarimana yararashwe. Abari bayirimo bose barapfa. Dusabye abantu bose kuguma mu rugo, kugeza aho tugiriye andi makuru.*

[‹Hier soir, l'avion transportant le président de la république Juvénal Habyarimana a été abattu. Il n'y a eu aucun survivant. Nous vous prions tous de rester chez vous, jusqu'à ce qu'on ait plus de nouvelles.›]

JEUNE EDDY   Le jour, la milice chasse, poursuit, guillotine.

La nuit, la guérilla descend les milles collines.

Le ciel est parsemé d'étoiles rouges

L'air est fracassé par des explosions sourdes.

Un matin, un des murs de la maison
Est criblé de trous de petite dimension.
Ç'a dû être une grenade.
Sommes pas armés, sommes en rade
Et donc, à part Papa qui est malade
Nous passons les nuits dans le corridor.

Conscience arrête la bande.

CONSCIENCE Dans le corridor d'une villa... Alors que tout autour d'eux, des gens sont traqués par des milices à la machette et charcutés à mort... Tu vois, c'est ça mon problème. Il était peut-être 'témoin' d'un génocide mais il n'en est pas un 'survivant'. Il n'était même pas ciblé par les tueries.

VANITÉ Écoutons jusqu'au bout mon histoire et puis on peut discuter. Et cette fois, c'est toi qui la fermes et écoutes!

Il joue sa bande.

VANITÉ (*sur cassette*) Alors que la famille est assiégée, n'osant pas quitter la maison et passant la nuit au sol même entre les confins du corridor, George, aussi quinze ans, pote et voisin d'Eddy, ne laisse pas passer un jour sans rendre visite à Eddy et sa famille...

LES AMIS NE SONT PLUS

GEORGE Eddy!

JEUNE EDDY	George…!
GEORGE	*Bite*? [‹Comment ça va?›]
JEUNE EDDY	Ça va.
GEORGE	T'as entendu, par rapport à Cassius?
JEUNE EDDY	Non…
GEORGE	Il a été tué. Il s'est retrouvé face à des rebelles en dehors de chez lui. Et Victor, Edouard, Emile, Justin, Rose, Yvonne… Gisèle! Tous morts, tués par la milice.
JEUNE EDDY	Et David?
GEORGE	Ils ont déjà quitté le pays…
JEUNE EDDY	Et…

Pause.

GEORGE	Chris…? Des miliciens sont allés chez eux et ont arrosé toute la famille avec des balles.
JEUNE EDDY	J'savais même pas qu'ils étaient Tutsis…
GEORGE	Je ne pense pas qu'ils l'étaient… Je crois que c'était pour des raisons politiques… C'est fou, tant de gens en train de se faire tuer… Parfois par pure jalousie ou rancune… Le voisin t'accuse d'être Tutsi et t'es mort.
JEUNE EDDY	Ou parce que t'es beaux, riche, grand…
GEORGE	Ça veut pas dire que t'es Tutsi ça, mon frère est grand et il n'est pas Tutsi.
JEUNE EDDY	…Comment il va?
GEORGE	Il se chie dessus. N'ose pas quitter la baraque.

LE SECRET DE MAMAN

À la maison.

MAMAN   Eddy, où sont tes sœurs?

JEUNE EDDY   Jenny, Gabby et moi-même

Nous asseyons autour de Maman dans la salle à manger.

Papa dort.

Sa situation s'empire.

A perdu la voix

A perdu du poids

N'a plus la force de parler

Ni de se lever.

C'est donc bizarre

D'entendre ces histoires

De Papa draguant Maman les temps d'antan

Car c'est pour ça que Maman nous a réunis sur le banc:

Pour nous raconter l'histoire de Papa & Maman.

MAMAN   ...Et quand votre père a reçu la bourse pour étudier en Belgique, il est devenu une célébrité au village. Et dès lors, chaque fois qu'il venait me rendre visite, mes sœurs étaient jalouses... Lorsqu'on s'est marié il était toujours étudiant et nous sommes donc retournés ensemble en Belgique, où vous deux sont nés... Une fois là-bas, j'avais pas mal de nettoyage à faire:

votre papa avait eu quelques copines et avait conservé les photos, les lettres... tout.

JEUNE EDDY　Tout d'un coup

Maman change de sujet.

Maman

Dit

Qu'elle a été adoptée

Par un ami à son père

Quand son propre père est décédé.

Cet ami-là

– Grand-père! –

L'a enlevée de sa maman à elle.

Maman ne sait pas ce qu'est devenue sa maman

Elle ne l'a jamais revue.

MAMAN　Mon... Votre grand-père était riche et puissant, il était diplomate, avec deux femmes. Et à peu près quinze enfants tous compris. Il a donc décidé que je serais mieux avec lui, puisque je n'étais qu'une pauvre enfant Tutsie...

Pause.

JEUNE EDDY　Gabby, tu savais, toi, par rapport à Maman? T'avais pas l'air surprise.

GABBY　Je savais pas, mais ça m'a semblé logique.

JEUNE EDDY　Comment ça?

GABBY　T'as jamais remarqué qu'elle ne ressemblait du tout à aucune de nos tantes? Et de toute façon je me suis toujours sentie différente avec eux moi.

JEUNE EDDY Ouais, moi aussi, mais j'ai toujours pensé que c'était parce qu'on venait de Belgique.

P'TE JENNY De quoi est-ce que vous parlez vous deux?

GABBY Tu comprendrais pas Jenny, t'es trop jeune.

ÉTAT DE SIÈGE

JEUNE EDDY Rester à l'intérieur

N'est pas recommandé.

On peut te soupçonner

De n'importe quoi

N'importe quand

N'importe comment.

Papa...

Peut rien accomplir.

Maman...

Doit pas sortir!

C'est donc moi

Le seul homme sous le toit

L'ainé de la famille

L'homme de la famille

Prêt au sacrifice

Qui prend les risques
Et s'aventure dehors.

Rue.

GÉRARD   Eddy we! *Bite*?

JEUNE EDDY   Je tombe sur Gérard.

Quinze ans
Tout comme moi
Pourtant je suis effrayé.
Il est défoncé
Avec une Kalashnikov en bandoulière.

GÉRARD   T'as entendu, ce qui est arrivé à Simba? *(Eddy fait non de la tête)* Nous sommes allés là-bas et on les a découpés. Oh, Simba s'est enfui, alors on l'a poursuivi au travers les buissons derrière leur maison... Et c'est moi qui l'ai attrapé! *(Éclate de rire)* Allez, achète-moi une bière...

JEUNE EDDY   Je... J'ai pas d'argent sur moi...

Le rire disparaît.

GÉRARD   Tu vas où en fait?

JEUNE EDDY   Je... suis juste en train de marcher...

Ses yeux
Défoncés
Avec une étincelle en plus
Me fixent...
Petit bourgeois
Plutôt beau
– Je tiens ça de ma maman –

Je remplis tous les critères!

Après un loong regard...

GÉRARD Je m'en vais au *kabare*. [‹bar›] *(Montrant du doigt sa Kalashnikov)* Je vais probablement pas devoir payer de toute façon. *(Éclate de rire)*

JEUNE EDDY Il semblerait que je ne remplisse pas tous les critères, tout compte fait. Ce doit être ma taille. Mon manque de hauteur.

ON CACHE, ON PART

GEORGE Eddy! Demain, nous partons. Avec vous. Je ne permettrai pas notre camionnette de démarrer sans ta famille. Dis-le à tes parents.

MAMAN *Bite* George?

GEORGE Je vais bien, Mama-Eddy, merci.

MAMAN Où est-ce que vous nous déposeriez?

GEORGE Nous allons chez mes grand-parents. On peut vous déposer où vous voulez au cours de la route.

MAMAN Eddy, Gabby, Jenny, rassemblez tout ce que vous avez de précieux.

La chambre d'Eddy. Il feuillète un album:

JEUNE EDDY Katia, Mireille, Nathalie... *(soupire)* Chris...

Mon album d'école...

(Le met de côté.

Va vers son lecteur. Il joue subitement une bande et se met à danser et chanter (à un mix de ses chansons favorites))

‹And Mac Daddy make it up! JUMP! Jump! Kris Kross make it up! Jump! Jump!›

‹BEAT IT! Beat it! Beat it! No one wants to be defeated! Aw!›

‹Although we've come to the END OF THE ROAD!›

(S'arrête tout aussi subitement) Et mes cassettes et mon lecteur... Et c'est tout. *(Les met de côté)*

Un trou dans le plafond

Je m'y faufile au plus profond

Et y range en plein milieu

Nos objets précieux.

GABBY   Est-ce qu'on va même passer la première barrière, Eddy? Maman devrait s'enlaidir. Là au moins on aurait une petite chance. Et la bonne, le gardien de nuit et leur petit garçon? Ils font quasiment parti de la famille maintenant. Est-ce qu'il y aura de la place pour eux dans la voiture?

JEUNE EDDY   J'en sais rien, Gabby!

La camionnette est un pick-up à cinq sièges.

Mère a convaincu Père:

MAMAN   Nous irons jusqu'à la prochaine ville, pas plus loin.

Nous ne pouvons pas rester, dans tous les cas.

PAPA Aide-moi à me lever, dans ce cas...

JEUNE EDDY C'est donc moi et maman

À chacun de ses flancs.

Il agonise

Les autres sympathisent

Il s'installe.

Siège arrière:

Papa, Maman, P'te Jenny, la maman de George.

Maman ne veut qu'une chose: qu'elle disparaisse.

Siège passager:

Le grand-frère de George.

Qui voudrait être plus petit qu'il ne paraisse.

Siège chauffeur:

George.

Pas un de ses grand-frères.

George.

Dans le plateau derrière:

Le reste de sa famille et leurs objets précieux

Gabby et moi sommes assis parmi eux.

Notre bonne et gardien de nuit et leur petit garçon

...Resteront.

Et garderont la maison jusqu'à notre retour.

Rue.

JEUNE EDDY   Barrière.

Des cadavres sur les côtés.

Étaient-ils grands?

Étaient-ils riches?

Étaient-ils beaux?

Était-il marqué 'Tutsi' dans leur carte d'identité?

Ils ont été découpés par les miliciens.

Qui se mettent à inspecter l'arrière.

Et à inspecter l'avant.

MILICIEN   MUGIYE   HE?   MURIMO MURAHUNGA   IKI?!   KUKI MUHUNGA KIGALI? [‹Vous allez où? Qu'est-ce que vous fuyez? Pourquoi fuyez-vous Kigali?›]

IDANTITE! [‹Cartes d'identité!›]

JEUNE EDDY   Il manque un document, est-ce qu'il sait compter?

Le Milicien rend les documents. Il s'aperçoit alors de la maman d'Eddy. Il lui montre du doigt.

MILICIEN   *Uriya. Hanze.* [‹Celle-là. Dehors.›]

JEUNE EDDY   Heureusement que je ne peux pas voir Maman de là où je suis placé

La terreur doit être en train de lui défigurer la beauté...

George

Le Gosse

Intervient.

GEORGE Son mari est en train de mourir... Regarde par toi-même...

Le Milicien se penche vers le siège arrière.

MILICIEN *Hanze.* [‹Dehors.›]

JEUNE EDDY Maman se précipite dans son sac-à-main et en déniche tout billet et pièce d'argent qu'elle possède. D'une main d'expert George les passe au milicien, personne d'autre n'a vu, et le milicien veut tout pour lui-même...

MILICIEN *(riant, à ses compères)* ABA BA HUTU BAHUNGA! BAKANGA NO GUKORA AKAZI NKATWE! [‹Ces Hutus qui s'enfuient ! Qui ne veulent même pas «travailler», comme nous!›]

(Aux passagers) MUGENDE! [‹Partez!›]

Il lève la barrière.

Conscience arrête la bande.

CONSCIENCE Comment est-ce qu'ils ont laissé Maman en vie...? Même aujourd'hui, je ne comprends toujours pas... Pourquoi est-ce qu'ils ne l'ont pas sortie de la voiture, violée et tuée comme tous les autres dont les corps étaient empilés sur les côtés?

VANITÉ C'est comme si tu aurais aimé qu'elle eut été tuée ce jour-là... Ah, tu te serais senti comme un vrai survivant du génocide dans ce cas-là, c'est ça?

CONSCIENCE   Sois pas ridicule... C'est quand même bizarre, non? Tu t'es jamais posé la question?

VANITÉ   Le pognon. Ce doit être le pognon.

CONSCIENCE   Nan... L'argent n'aurait dû lui acheter qu'une balle dans la tête à la place d'un coup de machette dans la nuque... Rappelle-toi de nos voisins... Ils étaient encore plus riches que nous...

VANITÉ   Papa ressemblait déjà à un cadavre... Ils ont peut-être eu pitié de nous...

CONSCIENCE   Des miliciens qui ont pitié? Tu te fous de ma gueule...? Je suppose que c'était de la chance. Une intervention de Dieu, Imana, Allah, Jehovah... quel que soit son nom. Et c'est exactement ce que je veux dire. C'est soit l'argent, soit l'aide du voisin, soit de la chance pure et simple. Eddy n'a, au fait, pas vu la Mort dans les yeux.

VANITÉ   ...D'accord.

Et si on continuait avec mes souvenirs? Ça te dérangerait pas...?

Il joue la bande.

VANITÉ *(sur cassette)* George nous dépose dans la ville voisine de Gitarama et ils reprennent le chemin.

Les au revoir sont brefs, on se reverra bientôt, c'est certain.

PARADIS PERDU

Enceinte clôturée.

JEUNE EDDY Notre hôte pendant les jours qui viennent
Est une amie de la famille, une politicienne.
Nous sommes une cohorte de famille et amis
Tous rescapés de tueurs et bandits.

L'un des garçons est grand et magnifique
Ce qui va rendre ma tâche problématique
Car les filles sont toutes des beautés de la République
Interdites de se montrer en public.

Naomi sort du lot...

Naomi, mon élixir!
La regarder est plus qu'un plaisir!
Elle a sept ans de plus que moi, j'ai pu saisir
Ce qui ne fait que renforcer mon désir!

Naomi et moi, et les autres couples
Flirtons...
Jouons aux dames...
En flirtant...
Allons puiser de l'eau à la source

> Les hommes aussi bien que les dames.
>
> C'est romantique
>
> C'est fantastique
>
> C'est hédoniste
>
> C'est– *(Explosions lointaines)*
>
> Des feux d'artifice! Là-bas, au sommet de la colline!
>
> Nous sommes jeunes et fou amoureux...
>
> Nous fonçons donc vers le sommet de la colline!

Sommet de la colline.

NAOMI   Eddy we? Tu es où?

JEUNE EDDY *(lui jouait un tour)* Ha ha, ici, Naomi, tiens, tiens ma main. *(Ils se faufilent dans la foule...)* Excusez-moi, monsieur...

SPECTATEUR #1 *EY! Aba bana ra! Murimo murasunikira iki?* [‹Eh! Ces gosses! À quoi bon bousculer?›]

JEUNE EDDY   On veut juste aller devant pour voir, on est jeunes et petits... Viens, Naomi. *(Force son chemin)* Excusez-moi, monsieur...

SPECTATEUR #2 *Ey! Ubu se murakora iki hano?? Mutahe, mutahe... Abana b'ubu rwose...* [‹Eh! Qu'est-ce que vous foutez ici?? Rentrez, rentrez... Les jeunes d'aujourd'hui vraiment...›]

JEUNE EDDY   Mais pourquoi? On veut juste–

NAOMI   Eddy, peut-être qu'on devrait juste rester là...

JEUNE EDDY   Non! T'arrive à voir quelque chose, toi, d'ici? Moi non plus. Allons devant. Et voyons à quoi est dû ce tap– *(Ils sont devant)*

La cour de l'église.

Pleine.

De corps.

Vieux, femmes, enfants, bébés, morts.

La fumée traîne encore dans l'air telle de la vapeur

Résultat de grenades lancées parmi ces victimes de l'injustice.

Elle est cisaillée par le regard noir des tueurs

Qui maraudent encore entre les corps au supplice

À la recherche

De ce gémissement

De ce tressaillement

Qui trahirait un corps comme étant encore vivant.

Naomi et moi regardons. Comment? Pourquoi?

Une femme avec un bébé a bougé.

Non!! Bouge pas, gémis pas, résiste ta douleur!!

Un vieil homme lève une main

En supplication

Un tueur prend la main du vieux.

La tranche.

La brandit à la foule.

Charcute le reste du corps.

Le bébé de la femme se met à pleurer.

Le tueur interrompt le découpage du vieux et se dirige vers la femme et le bébé.

Sa machette monte–

JEUNE EDDY   Naomi et moi reforçons notre chemin au travers la foule–

SPECTATEUR #3 *Aba bana barwaye iki ra?!* [‹Mais qu'est-ce qu'ils ont ces gosses?!›]

JEUNE EDDY   Et redescendons la colline en courant.

PERTE ET BAUME

JEUNE EDDY   La vie au village continue comme naguère.

Cousin Luc me sort prendre un verre.

Lorsqu'un messager nous retrouve au bar

Nous abandonnons nos calebasses et rentrons dans le noir.

On y est presque, Cousin Luc est pratiquement en train de courir

Des chants nous parviennent, le vent osant à peine les couvrir.

Dans l'enceinte.

Maman est assise, entourée de femmes qui chantent.

Papa...

Son lit occupe toute la pièce.

Son corps est illuminé par une bougie au coin de l'aile.

Peu importe cette tristesse

Je touche son visage, il est froid, je chancèle...

Il est vraiment parti. Quels étaient ses derniers mots

A-t-il parlé?

Je suis enivré – par ce chant funèbre

Ignore le chant!

Trouve Maman

Un moment avec ma maman

Au lieu de Maman, je trouve Naomi.

La nuit où j'ai perdu mon géniteur
La nuit où j'ai perdu ma fleur.

LAISSANT TOUT DERRIÈRE SOI

Voiture.

JEUNE EDDY Nous abandonnons tout, Papa y compris

J'abandonne tout, y compris Naomi

                Nous arrivons sur le grand boulevard

                Cousin Luc s'arrête et se gare

COUSIN LUC   Réfléchissons...

                Eh... Prions et préparons-nous...

JEUNE EDDY   Cousin Luc qui est grand et Maman qui est belle... Y a qu'un miracle qui puisse sauver la mise...

Une voiture arrive à toute vitesse et freine avec crissement.

                Le Parrain!

                Qui peut aller partout sans problèmes!

                Y a qu'à voir sa caisse – ses fringues même!

                Sort toujours de nulle part

                L'homme de sauvetage!

En route.

JEUNE EDDY   Barrière

                Les miliciens dansent, se pavanent.

                Le Parrain

                Enfonce le klaxon

                Baisse la vitre

                Et hurle

LE PARRAIN   ZAMURA IYO BARIYERI CYANGWA MBINJIREMO MWESE! [‹Levez cette barrière ou je fonce dedans!›]

JEUNE EDDY   Il crie plus fort que son klaxon

                C'est pas crier

                C'est aboyer

LE PARRAIN   WOOF! WOOF! WOOF! WOOF! WOOF!! ABA BASWERA NYINA

NTIBUMVA RA? HAWUSIKILIYE?? ZAMURA IYO BARIYERI!! [‹Ces enculés ne comprennent pas ou quoi?? Vous me comprenez ou pas?? Enlevez cette barrière!!›]

JEUNE EDDY   Ralentit pas.

Mon Cousin

Encore moins.

Va y avoir un carnage.

Par-dessus l'autre carnage.

Et puis... comme ça... ils dégagent la voie!

Ouah... C'est comme ça qu'on aurait dû faire depuis tout ce temps?

Enceinte clôturée.

L'EXODE

JEUNE EDDY   Nous rejoignons la grande famille chez les grand-parents

À Gisenyi

Et tous ensemble

Ne sommes plus que partie infime d'une masse

Débordant des frontières qui l'entasse.

On campe

À Goma

On reste ensemble

À Goma.

La nouvelle milice

Que sont le choléra et la dysenterie

Attaque notre colonie

Tue et nous garde en esclavage

Garde ma tante et moi-même en otage.

Elle est sous perfusion

Moi sur grosse commission

Je chie mon sang chère

Je transpire ma chaire

Y a plus que mes os qui me tiennent raide.

Ils épargnent P'te Jenny

Pourtant sujette aux maladies

Et ignorent Maman et Gabby.

Je survis.

Vanité arrête la bande.

CONSCIENCE D'accord... d'accord. Je l'admet. Ce n'était pas une petite promenade.

VANITÉ Et le privilège et l'argent et toutes ces conneries... Rien à voir.

CONSCIENCE En effet, en effet... Rien à voir...

VANITÉ Aha!

CONSCIENCE Mais... Ça ne lui donne toujours pas le droit de se prendre pour une victime...

VANITÉ Mon dieu, mais qu'est-ce que t'es têtu!

CONSCIENCE Ah oui? Vraiment...? Okay, une fois à Goma, qui est-ce qu'on est tombé dessus? Je me demande si tu te souviens de ça, tiens...

Il joue la bande...

Rue.

CHRIS *(sur cassette)* Edmundoooo!!

JEUNE EDDY Impossible. Je regarde à gauche, à droite, devant et derrière mais vois rien.

CHRIS Edmundoooo!!

JEUNE EDDY Est-ce possible? Dans le fourgon, là-bas, au-dessus du tas, me faisant signe de la main?

CHRIS Je descends au coin de la rue!!

JEUNE EDDY Je cours après le fourgon pour le garder en pleine vue. Il tourne, je l'ai perdu. Plus vite!! Je tourne... Pas de fourgon.

CHRIS Edmundo!!

JEUNE EDDY C'est bien lui.

Chris.

Mon frère.

Il traverse la rue

En courant

En souriant

On saute dans les bras l'un de l'autre.

CHRIS Ouah! Tu t'en es sorti toi aussi fieux!

JEUNE EDDY *(à lui-même)* Mais comment?! Mais comment!! Comment.

CHRIS Écoute fieux, je suis en contact avec des amis de famille en Allemagne...

J'y vais bientôt. Et toi, comment ça se passe?

JEUNE EDDY Maman est en contact avec mon oncle en Belgique. Il essaie de nous amener là-bas.

On ne trouve pas nos mots.

Éventuellement

Car il a dû lire ma curiosité dans les yeux

Il me raconte.

CHRIS Nous étions tous dans le salon quand ils sont arrivés. Enfin, moi j'y étais pas, j'étais aux toilettes. Ils ont dû être pressés parce qu'ils n'ont pas fouillé la maison après... leur besogne. Je suis resté encore presqu'une semaine avant de me décider à partir. À pied. Quoique j'ai parfois fait du stop. Je suis arrivé ici à Goma il y a deux semaines et la première chose que j'ai faite était de me trouver un téléphone...

Conscience arrête la bande.

CONSCIENCE Il est vrai que Chris venait, lui aussi, d'un milieu privilégié, mais lui, il a absolument tout perdu, y compris sa famille entière. Eddy, par contre, avait encore sa famille après le génocide. Et Papa ne compte pas, il n'a pas été tué, il est mort de maladie. Il serait mort de toute façon.

VANITÉ Tant d'efforts pour qu'Eddy se sente coupable d'avoir survécu le génocide.

CONSCIENCE Tant d'efforts pour qu'Eddy se sente fière d'avoir été témoin du génocide.

VANITÉ Je suis sa vanité, c'est mon boulot.

CONSCIENCE Et moi sa conscience.

VANITÉ Exactement! Et t'es sensé le guider! Et pas d'apparaître à chaque fois qu'il joue son histoire d'amour entre un black et une blanche qui se rencontrent dans une boîte à Paris! Il n'est jamais arrivé à la fin de cette pièce. Jamais! Le gars doit passer à autre chose...

CONSCIENCE Écoute, je comprends ta frustration. Mais, honnêtement, je crois qu'Eddy doit apprendre à apprécier ce qu'il lui a été donné. Il vit maintenant en Europe, où il a reçu une excellente éducation, où il peut devenir ce qu'il veut – le mec est un acteur bon sang! Donc, autant que je déteste devoir le dire, Eddy est, en réalité, un... bénéficiaire du génocide – plus q'autre chose. Et pour le reste... Il passera à autre chose... Si lui, et nous, acceptons de laisser le temps au Temps de faire son boulot.

(À Eddy) T'as entendu, Eddy...? Eddy! T'as entendu ce que je viens de dire...? ED–

Eddy secoue Conscience et Vanité hors de lui.

Il est toujours dans son one-man show – son «histoire d'amour entre une blanche et un black qui se rencontrent dans une boîte à Paris» – en train de danser avec Chloé (début de la pièce).

Quoiqu'il se soit débarrassé de ses voix intérieurs, il est toujours perdu dans ses pensées, ou plutôt, dans son passé...

Cette fois-ci, ce sont ses souvenirs à lui...

LES SOUVENIRS DÉTERRÉS

JEUNE EDDY   Belgique.

Une semaine que nous sommes arrivés!

Une semaine de nuits ensoleillés!

Une semaine sans plus de déprime!

Une semaine pleine de primes!

Ouais, j'ai pris dix kilogrammes!

Une grossesse haut de gamme!

Le Centre de Demandeurs d'Asile:

Nouveau refuge, nouveau domicile!

Et mes confrères demandeurs d'asile:

Ma nouvelle famille!

La pièce familiale.

Moi, Maman, Gabby

– Mais où est P'te Jenny? –

Prenons place sur le velours.

Maman nous caresse la chevelure.

MAMAN   Jenny et moi avons le SIDA. Ça faisait longtemps que je le soupçonnais et maintenant des examens ont confirmé que nous sommes séropositives.

JEUNE EDDY Maman et Jenny sont en train de mourir?

Pourquoi?

Comment?

Papa!

Mais Jenny a huit ans

Comment aurait-elle pu vivre aussi longtemps?

Et Goma

Le choléra

Comment a-t-elle – comment ont-elles survécu?

Pourquoi nous?

Pourquoi Jenny?

Papa!

Maman pleure.

Gabby pleure.

Je...

Mais où sont donc mes larmes?

Combien de temps jusqu'à...?

C'est un compte à rebours.

VIVRE CONTRE LA MONTRE

JEUNE EDDY　Vacances d'été et je bosse sur une ferme, loin de l'Asile.

Maman est fière de me voir bosser pour la première fois de ma vie.

Le Centre de Demandeurs d'Asile.

> J'ai avec moi
>
> Les patins à roulettes grises
>
> Que Jenny a toujours aimés.
>
> Je la vois
>
> Au travers le portail et sa grille
>
> Elle est en train de compter.
>
> Elle me voit
>
> Arrête son compte
>
> Appelle mon nom
>
> Court vers moi
>
> Tout sourire
>
> Saute dans mes bras
>
> Et je la serre
>
> Fort.
>
> Elle est plus légère.
>
> Tout mince, son corps.

L'EXCURSION

AMI DE MAMAN　Ça vous dirait une petite excursion à Bruxelles?

JEUNE EDDY   Un ami que Maman a rencontré à l'hôpital – elle était fort malade

Veut nous emmener faire une petite ballade.

Il veut rendre les derniers jours de Maman sur terre les plus joyeux possibles.

J'aime pas.

Cela me rappelle que Maman est en train de vivre ses derniers jours sur terre.

J'irai pas.

Et donc P'te Jenny, Gabby et Maman

Visitent nos anciennes écoles, adresses et monuments

Et reviennent avec photos et épanouissement.

LE PREMIER COUP D'HORLOGE

En classe.

SECRÉTAIRE SCOLAIRE Bonjour tout le monde...

JEUNE EDDY   Je suis en classe et le Secrétaire vient d'entrer.

SECRÉTAIRE SCOLAIRE Mr André... J'aurais besoin de parler à Eddy en privé, s'il vous plaît.

JEUNE EDDY   Je suis debout. Adossé contre le mur. J'attends.

SECRÉTAIRE SCOLAIRE Euh... Eddy...

JEUNE EDDY   Je ne voudrais pas être à sa place.

SECRÉTAIRE SCOLAIRE Eddy... Ta maman vient de nous quitter. Y a ton oncle qui va venir te chercher. Vaudrait mieux que tu sois prêt quand il arrive. Je vais récupérer tes affaires en classe, d'accord? Ça va, Eddy...?

Le Centre de Demandeurs d'Asile.

JEUNE EDDY   Je regarde les photos.

Gabby, Jenny, Maman.

Ses derniers jours.

Et je ne suis pas là.

N'étais pas là pour les derniers jours de Papa.

N'étais pas là pour les derniers jours de Maman.

Mais où elles sont ces larmes?!

LE DERNIER COUP DE L'HORLOGE

JEUNE EDDY   Le compte à rebours continue son décompte.

P'te Jenny ne peut plus rouler avec ses patins.

Hôpital.

Elle ne peut plus quitter son lit d'hôsto.

La maladie la ronge, sous ses draps je devine ses os.

Pourtant nous discutons et parlons sérieusement

On dirait une adulte, elle parle différemment

Comme si son cerveau avait décidé d'aller plus vite

Pour lui donner ces années qui lui sont interdites.

(À Jenny et Gabby) J'ai besoin d'aller aux toilettes, je reviens tout-de-suite.

P'TE JENNY Tu aurais pu utiliser ma toilette mais l'hôpital stipule que les visiteurs et patients ne doivent pas partager la même toilette.

JEUNE EDDY Je sais, je sais. J'en trouverai une autre.

P'TE JENNY Il y en a une au fond du couloir à ta droite.

Toilette.

JEUNE EDDY Je tire la chasse et évacue toutes mes larmes.

Ces larmes que je n'arrivais pas à trouver

Voilà pourquoi.

C'était pour maintenant que je les avais gardées.

De retour dans la chambre de Jenny.

Hé... me revoilà.

GABBY   Jenny disait que tu prends toujours des plombes aux toilettes... Eh ben elle avait raison...!

JEUNE EDDY Elles rient.

Toutes les deux.

Cent-cinquante jours après le départ de Maman

P'te Jenny en a marre de la lutte et rejoint Papa et Maman.

Le compte à rebours s'arrête à six-cent-deux jours.

Elle avait neuf ans.

ICI & MAINTENANT

Les souvenirs d'Eddy s'arrêtent.

Il s'est perdu dans son passé et a oublié son one-man show...

Il va au lecteur, retire les souvenirs de Conscience et de Vanité (cassettes).

Il se rend compte de la présence du public et décide alors de relancer le one-man show. Il rembobine sa propre cassette (celle du show) jusqu'au début, et joue.

Le dernier tube s'échappe des enceintes...

Une boîte. Eddy impressionne Chloé avec ses pas de danse.

CHLOÉ *(rie)* Ouah! Non, mais, t'es un vrai génie de la danse, toi!

EDDY Merci!

CHLOÉ Au fait... Tu viens d'où?

EDDY De La Chapelle. Et toi?

CHLOÉ De La Villette.

EDDY Ah bon, mais on est pratiquement voisins...! Tu prends le métro tout-à-l'heure?

CHLOÉ (*sourit*) Peut-être... (*Un petit moment de danse gênée et timide. Puis–*) Au fait, je voulais dire, tu viens d'où d'origine?

EDDY (*comprend*) Ah, de Belgique.

Noir.

Fin.

Aurora Metro Books

HAMLET adapted by Mark Norfolk
ISBN 978-911501-01-5   £9.99

COMBUSTION by Asif Khan
ISBN 978-1-911501-91-6   £9.99

DIARY OF A HOUNSLOW GIRL by Ambreen Razia
ISBN 978-0-9536757-9-1   £8.99

SPLIT/MIXED by Ery Nzaramba
ISBN 978-1-911501-97-8   £10.99

A GIRL WITH A BOOK by Nick Wood
ISBN 978-1-9107898-61-4   £12.99

THE TROUBLE WITH ASIAN MEN by Sudha Bhuchar, Kristine Landon-Smith and Louise Wallinger
ISBN 978-1-906582-41-8   £8.99

SOUTHEAST ASIAN PLAYS ed. Cheryl Robson and Aubrey Mellor
ISBN 978-1-906582-86-9   £16.99

SIX PLAYS BY BLACK AND ASIAN WOMEN WRITERS ed. Kadija George
ISBN 978-0-9515877-2-0   £12.99

DURBAN DIALOGUES, INDIAN VOICE by Ashwin Singh
ISBN 978-1-906582-42-5   £15.99

WOMEN OF ASIA by Asa Palomera
ISBN 978-1-906582-94-4   £7.99

HARVEST by Manjula Padmanabhan
ISBN 978-0-9536757-7-7   £6.99

I HAVE BEFORE ME A REMARKABLE DOCUMENT by Sonja Linden
ISBN 978-09546912-3-3   £7.99

THE IRANIAN FEAST by Kevin Dyer
ISBN 978-1-910798-93-5   £8.99

NEW SOUTH AFRICAN PLAYS ed. Charles J. Fourie
ISBN 978-0-9542330-1-3   £11. 99

BLACK AND ASIAN PLAYS Anthology introduced by Afia Nkrumah
ISBN 978-0-9536757-4-6   £12. 99

www.aurorametro.com